MW00654235

MOVIES TO CHECK OUT

[A Do-It-Yourself Movie Guide]

CHRONICLE BOOKS
SAN FRANCISCO

MOVIES TO SEE

The length of a film should be directly related to the endurance of the human bladder.

—ALFRED HITCHCOCK

[MOVIES TO SEE]

[MOVIES TO SEE]

_____

_____

_____

_____

_____

_____

_____

_____

_____

_____

_____

_____

_____

_____

_____

_____

_____

_____

_____

_____

_____

_____

[MOVIES TO SEE]

[MOVIES TO SEE]

[MOVIES TO SEE]

[MOVIES TO SEE]

[MOVIES TO SEE]

[MOVIES TO SEE]

[MOVIES TO SEE]

_____

_____

_____

_____

_____

_____

_____

_____

_____

_____

_____

_____

_____

_____

_____

_____

_____

_____

_____

[MOVIES TO SEE]

[MOVIES TO SEE]

[MOVIES TO SEE]

[MOVIES TO SEE]

[MOVIES TO SEE]

[MOVIES TO SEE]

[MOVIES TO SEE]

[MOVIES TO SEE]

[MOVIES TO SEE]

[MOVIES TO SEE]

[MOVIES TO SEE]

MOVIE REVIEWS

Never judge a movie by its book.

—J. W. EAGAN

[MOVIE REVIEWS]

TITLE:

_____

DIRECTED BY:

_____

STARRING:

_____

_____

GENRE:

__ drama __ comedy __ romance __ action

__ horror __ sci-fi/fantasy __ foreign __ other

SEE IT:

__ at the theater __ at home

RATING:

__* __** __*** __**** __*****

AWARDS:

deserved: _____

_____

received: _____

_____

[MOVIE REVIEWS]

TITLE:

_____

DIRECTED BY:

_____

STARRING:

_____

_____

GENRE:

__ drama __ comedy __ romance __ action

__ horror __ sci-fi/fantasy __ foreign __ other

SEE IT:

__ at the theater __ at home

RATING:

__* __** __*** __**** __*****

AWARDS:

deserved: _____

_____

received: _____

_____

[MOVIE REVIEWS]

TITLE:

_____

DIRECTED BY:

_____

STARRING:

_____

_____

GENRE:

__ drama __ comedy __ romance __ action

__ horror __ sci-fi/fantasy __ foreign __ other

SEE IT:

__ at the theater __ at home

RATING:

__* __** __*** __**** __*****

AWARDS:

deserved: _____

_____

received: _____

_____

[MOVIE REVIEWS]

TITLE:

_____

DIRECTED BY:

_____

STARRING:

_____

_____

GENRE:

__ drama __ comedy __ romance __ action

__ horror __ sci-fi/fantasy __ foreign __ other

SEE IT:

__ at the theater __ at home

RATING:

__* __** __*** __**** __*****

AWARDS:

deserved: _____

_____

received: _____

_____

[MOVIE REVIEWS]

TITLE:

_____

DIRECTED BY:

_____

STARRING:

_____

_____

GENRE:

__ drama __ comedy __ romance __ action

__ horror __ sci-fi/fantasy __ foreign __ other

SEE IT:

__ at the theater __ at home

RATING:

__* __** __*** __**** __*****

AWARDS:

deserved: _____

_____

received: _____

_____

[MOVIE REVIEWS]

TITLE:

_____

DIRECTED BY:

_____

STARRING:

_____

_____

GENRE:

__ drama   __ comedy   __ romance   __ action

__ horror   __ sci-fi/fantasy   __ foreign   __ other

SEE IT:

__ at the theater   __ at home

RATING:

__*   __**   __***   __****   __*****

AWARDS:

deserved: _____

_____

received: _____

_____

[MOVIE REVIEWS]

TITLE:

_____

DIRECTED BY:

_____

STARRING:

_____

_____

GENRE:

__ drama __ comedy __ romance __ action

__ horror __ sci-fi/fantasy __ foreign __ other

SEE IT:

__ at the theater __ at home

RATING:

__* __** __*** __**** __*****

AWARDS:

deserved: _____

_____

received: _____

_____

[MOVIE REVIEWS]

TITLE:

_____

DIRECTED BY:

_____

STARRING:

_____

_____

GENRE:

__ drama __ comedy __ romance __ action

__ horror __ sci-fi/fantasy __ foreign __ other

SEE IT:

__ at the theater __ at home

RATING:

__* __** __*** __**** __*****

AWARDS:

deserved: _____

_____

received: _____

_____

[MOVIE REVIEWS]

TITLE:

_____

DIRECTED BY:

_____

STARRING:

_____

_____

GENRE:

__ drama __ comedy __ romance __ action

__ horror __ sci-fi/fantasy __ foreign __ other

SEE IT:

__ at the theater __ at home

RATING:

__* __** __*** __**** __*****

AWARDS:

deserved: _____

_____

received: _____

_____

[MOVIE REVIEWS]

TITLE:

_____

DIRECTED BY:

_____

STARRING:

_____

_____

GENRE:

__ drama __ comedy __ romance __ action

__ horror __ sci-fi/fantasy __ foreign __ other

SEE IT:

__ at the theater __ at home

RATING:

__* __** __*** __**** __*****

AWARDS:

deserved: _____

_____

received: _____

_____

[MOVIE REVIEWS]

TITLE:

_____

DIRECTED BY:

_____

STARRING:

_____

_____

GENRE:

__ drama __ comedy __ romance __ action

__ horror __ sci-fi/fantasy __ foreign __ other

SEE IT:

__ at the theater __ at home

RATING:

__* __** __*** __**** __*****

AWARDS:

deserved: _____

_____

received: _____

_____

[MOVIE REVIEWS]

TITLE:

_____

DIRECTED BY:

_____

STARRING:

_____

_____

GENRE:

__ drama __ comedy __ romance __ action

__ horror __ sci-fi/fantasy __ foreign __ other

SEE IT:

__ at the theater __ at home

RATING:

__* __** __*** __**** __*****

AWARDS:

deserved: _____

_____

received: _____

_____

[MOVIE REVIEWS]

TITLE:

_____

DIRECTED BY:

_____

STARRING:

_____

_____

GENRE:

__ drama __ comedy __ romance __ action

__ horror __ sci-fi/fantasy __ foreign __ other

SEE IT:

__ at the theater __ at home

RATING:

__* __** __*** __**** __*****

AWARDS:

deserved: _____

_____

received: _____

_____

[MOVIE REVIEWS]

TITLE:

_____

DIRECTED BY:

_____

STARRING:

_____

_____

GENRE:

__ drama   __ comedy   __ romance   __ action

__ horror   __ sci-fi/fantasy   __ foreign   __ other

SEE IT:

__ at the theater   __ at home

RATING:

__* __** __*** __**** __*****

AWARDS:

deserved: _____

_____

received: _____

_____

[MOVIE REVIEWS]

TITLE:

_____

DIRECTED BY:

_____

STARRING:

_____

_____

GENRE:

__ drama __ comedy __ romance __ action

__ horror __ sci-fi/fantasy __ foreign __ other

SEE IT:

__ at the theater __ at home

RATING:

__* __** __*** __**** __*****

AWARDS:

deserved: _____

_____

received: _____

_____

[MOVIE REVIEWS]

TITLE:

_____

DIRECTED BY:

_____

STARRING:

_____

_____

GENRE:

__ drama __ comedy __ romance __ action

__ horror __ sci-fi/fantasy __ foreign __ other

SEE IT:

__ at the theater __ at home

RATING:

__* __** __*** __**** __*****

AWARDS:

deserved: _____

_____

received: _____

_____

[MOVIE REVIEWS]

TITLE:

_____

DIRECTED BY:

_____

STARRING:

_____

_____

GENRE:

__ drama __ comedy __ romance __ action

__ horror __ sci-fi/fantasy __ foreign __ other

SEE IT:

__ at the theater __ at home

RATING:

__* __** __*** __**** __*****

AWARDS:

deserved: _____

_____

received: _____

_____

[MOVIE REVIEWS]

TITLE:

_____

DIRECTED BY:

_____

STARRING:

_____

_____

GENRE:

__ drama __ comedy __ romance __ action

__ horror __ sci-fi/fantasy __ foreign __ other

SEE IT:

__ at the theater __ at home

RATING:

__* __** __*** __**** __*****

AWARDS:

deserved: _____

_____

received: _____

_____

[MOVIE REVIEWS]

TITLE:

DIRECTED BY:

STARRING:

GENRE:

__ drama __ comedy __ romance __ action

__ horror __ sci-fi/fantasy __ foreign __ other

SEE IT:

__ at the theater __ at home

RATING:

__* __** __*** __**** __*****

AWARDS:

deserved: _____

_____

received: _____

_____

[MOVIE REVIEWS]

TITLE:

_____

DIRECTED BY:

_____

STARRING:

_____

_____

GENRE:

__ drama __ comedy __ romance __ action

__ horror __ sci-fi/fantasy __ foreign __ other

SEE IT:

__ at the theater __ at home

RATING:

__* __** __*** __**** __*****

AWARDS:

deserved: _____

_____

received: _____

_____

[MOVIE REVIEWS]

TITLE:

_____

DIRECTED BY:

_____

STARRING:

_____

_____

GENRE:

__ drama __ comedy __ romance __ action

__ horror __ sci-fi/fantasy __ foreign __ other

SEE IT:

__ at the theater __ at home

RATING:

__* __** __*** __**** __*****

AWARDS:

deserved: _____

_____

received: _____

_____

[MOVIE REVIEWS]

TITLE:

_____

DIRECTED BY:

_____

STARRING:

_____

_____

GENRE:

__ drama   __ comedy   __ romance   __ action

__ horror   __ sci-fi/fantasy   __ foreign   __ other

SEE IT:

__ at the theater   __ at home

RATING:

__*   __**   __***   __****   __*****

AWARDS:

deserved: _____

_____

received: _____

_____

[MOVIE REVIEWS]

TITLE:

_____

DIRECTED BY:

_____

STARRING:

_____

_____

GENRE:

__ drama __ comedy __ romance __ action

__ horror __ sci-fi/fantasy __ foreign __ other

SEE IT:

__ at the theater __ at home

RATING:

__* __** __*** __**** __*****

AWARDS:

deserved: _____

_____

received: _____

_____

[MOVIE REVIEWS]

TITLE:

_____

DIRECTED BY:

_____

STARRING:

_____

_____

GENRE:

__ drama __ comedy __ romance __ action

__ horror __ sci-fi/fantasy __ foreign __ other

SEE IT:

__ at the theater __ at home

RATING:

__* __** __*** __**** __*****

AWARDS:

deserved: _____

_____

received: _____

_____

[MOVIE REVIEWS]

TITLE:

_____

DIRECTED BY:

_____

STARRING:

_____

_____

GENRE:

__ drama __ comedy __ romance __ action

__ horror __ sci-fi/fantasy __ foreign __ other

SEE IT:

__ at the theater __ at home

RATING:

__* __** __*** __**** __*****

AWARDS:

deserved: _____

_____

received: _____

_____

[MOVIE REVIEWS]

TITLE:

_____

DIRECTED BY:

_____

STARRING:

_____

_____

GENRE:

__ drama __ comedy __ romance __ action

__ horror __ sci-fi/fantasy __ foreign __ other

SEE IT:

__ at the theater __ at home

RATING:

__ * __ ** __ *** __ **** __ *****

AWARDS:

deserved: _____

_____

received: _____

_____

[MOVIE REVIEWS]

TITLE:

_____

DIRECTED BY:

_____

STARRING:

_____

_____

GENRE:

__ drama __ comedy __ romance __ action

__ horror __ sci-fi/fantasy __ foreign __ other

SEE IT:

__ at the theater __ at home

RATING:

__* __** __*** __**** __*****

AWARDS:

deserved: _____

_____

received: _____

_____

[MOVIE REVIEWS]

TITLE:

_____

DIRECTED BY:

_____

STARRING:

_____

_____

GENRE:

__ drama __ comedy __ romance __ action

__ horror __ sci-fi/fantasy __ foreign __ other

SEE IT:

__ at the theater __ at home

RATING:

__* __** __*** __**** __*****

AWARDS:

deserved: _____

_____

received: _____

_____

[MOVIE REVIEWS]

TITLE:

_____

DIRECTED BY:

_____

STARRING:

_____

_____

GENRE:

__ drama __ comedy __ romance __ action

__ horror __ sci-fi/fantasy __ foreign __ other

SEE IT:

__ at the theater __ at home

RATING:

__* __** __*** __**** __*****

AWARDS:

deserved: _____

_____

received: _____

_____

[MOVIE REVIEWS]

TITLE:

_____

DIRECTED BY:

_____

STARRING:

_____

_____

GENRE:

__ drama __ comedy __ romance __ action

__ horror __ sci-fi/fantasy __ foreign __ other

SEE IT:

__ at the theater __ at home

RATING:

__ *   __ **   __ ***   __ ****   __ *****

AWARDS:

deserved: _____

_____

received: _____

_____

[MOVIE REVIEWS]

TITLE:

_____

DIRECTED BY:

_____

STARRING:

_____

_____

GENRE:

__ drama __ comedy __ romance __ action

__ horror __ sci-fi/fantasy __ foreign __ other

SEE IT:

__ at the theater __ at home

RATING:

__* __** __*** __**** __*****

AWARDS:

deserved: _____

_____

received: _____

_____

[MOVIE REVIEWS]

TITLE:

_____

DIRECTED BY:

_____

STARRING:

_____

_____

GENRE:

__ drama __ comedy __ romance __ action

__ horror __ sci-fi/fantasy __ foreign __ other

SEE IT:

__ at the theater __ at home

RATING:

__* __** __*** __**** __*****

AWARDS:

deserved: _____

_____

received: _____

_____

[MOVIE REVIEWS]

TITLE:

_____

DIRECTED BY:

_____

STARRING:

_____

_____

GENRE:

__ drama __ comedy __ romance __ action

__ horror __ sci-fi/fantasy __ foreign __ other

SEE IT:

__ at the theater __ at home

RATING:

__★ __★★ __★★★ __★★★★ __★★★★★

AWARDS:

deserved: _____

_____

received: _____

_____

[MOVIE REVIEWS]

TITLE:

DIRECTED BY:

STARRING:

GENRE:

__ drama __ comedy __ romance __ action

__ horror __ sci-fi/fantasy __ foreign __ other

SEE IT:

__ at the theater __ at home

RATING:

__* __** __*** __**** __*****

AWARDS:

deserved: _____

_____

received: _____

_____

[MOVIE REVIEWS]

TITLE:

_____

DIRECTED BY:

_____

STARRING:

_____

_____

GENRE:

__ drama __ comedy __ romance __ action

__ horror __ sci-fi/fantasy __ foreign __ other

SEE IT:

__ at the theater __ at home

RATING:

__* __** __*** __**** __*****

AWARDS:

deserved: _____

_____

received: _____

_____

[MOVIE REVIEWS]

TITLE:

_____

DIRECTED BY:

_____

STARRING:

_____

_____

GENRE:

__ drama __ comedy __ romance __ action

__ horror __ sci-fi/fantasy __ foreign __ other

SEE IT:

__ at the theater __ at home

RATING:

__* __** __*** __**** __*****

AWARDS:

deserved: _____

_____

received: _____

_____

[MOVIE REVIEWS]

TITLE:

_____

DIRECTED BY:

_____

STARRING:

_____

_____

GENRE:

__ drama __ comedy __ romance __ action

__ horror __ sci-fi/fantasy __ foreign __ other

SEE IT:

__ at the theater __ at home

RATING:

__* __** __*** __**** __*****

AWARDS:

deserved: _____

_____

received: _____

_____

[MOVIE REVIEWS]

TITLE:

_____

DIRECTED BY:

_____

STARRING:

_____

_____

GENRE:

__ drama __ comedy __ romance __ action

__ horror __ sci-fi/fantasy __ foreign __ other

SEE IT:

__ at the theater __ at home

RATING:

__* __** __*** __**** __*****

AWARDS:

deserved: _____

_____

received: _____

_____

[MOVIE REVIEWS]

TITLE:

_____

DIRECTED BY:

_____

STARRING:

_____

_____

GENRE:

__ drama __ comedy __ romance __ action

__ horror __ sci-fi/fantasy __ foreign __ other

SEE IT:

__ at the theater __ at home

RATING:

__* __** __*** __**** __*****

AWARDS:

deserved: _____

_____

received: _____

_____

[MOVIE REVIEWS]

TITLE:

_____

DIRECTED BY:

_____

STARRING:

_____

_____

GENRE:

__ drama __ comedy __ romance __ action

__ horror __ sci-fi/fantasy __ foreign __ other

SEE IT:

__ at the theater __ at home

RATING:

__* __** __*** __**** __*****

AWARDS:

deserved: _____

_____

received: _____

_____

[MOVIE REVIEWS]

TITLE:

_____

DIRECTED BY:

_____

STARRING:

_____

_____

GENRE:

__ drama __ comedy __ romance __ action

__ horror __ sci-fi/fantasy __ foreign __ other

SEE IT:

__ at the theater __ at home

RATING:

__* __** __*** __**** __*****

AWARDS:

deserved: _____

_____

received: _____

_____

[MOVIE REVIEWS]

TITLE:

_____

DIRECTED BY:

_____

STARRING:

_____

_____

GENRE:

__ drama __ comedy __ romance __ action

__ horror __ sci-fi/fantasy __ foreign __ other

SEE IT:

__ at the theater __ at home

RATING:

__* __** __*** __**** __*****

AWARDS:

deserved: _____

_____

received: _____

_____

[MOVIE REVIEWS]

TITLE:

_____

DIRECTED BY:

_____

STARRING:

_____

_____

GENRE:

__ drama __ comedy __ romance __ action

__ horror __ sci-fi/fantasy __ foreign __ other

SEE IT:

__ at the theater __ at home

RATING:

__* __** __*** __**** __*****

AWARDS:

deserved: _____

_____

received: _____

_____

[MOVIE REVIEWS]

TITLE:

_____

DIRECTED BY:

_____

STARRING:

_____

_____

GENRE:

__ drama __ comedy __ romance __ action

__ horror __ sci-fi/fantasy __ foreign __ other

SEE IT:

__ at the theater __ at home

RATING:

__* __** __*** __**** __*****

AWARDS:

deserved: _____

_____

received: _____

_____

[MOVIE REVIEWS]

TITLE:

_____

DIRECTED BY:

_____

STARRING:

_____

_____

GENRE:

__ drama __ comedy __ romance __ action

__ horror __ sci-fi/fantasy __ foreign __ other

SEE IT:

__ at the theater __ at home

RATING:

__* __** __*** __**** __*****

AWARDS:

deserved: _____

_____

received: _____

_____

[MOVIE REVIEWS]

TITLE:

_____

DIRECTED BY:

_____

STARRING:

_____

_____

GENRE:

__ drama __ comedy __ romance __ action

__ horror __ sci-fi/fantasy __ foreign __ other

SEE IT:

__ at the theater __ at home

RATING:

__★ __★★ __★★★ __★★★★ __★★★★★

AWARDS:

deserved: _____

_____

received: _____

_____

[MOVIE REVIEWS]

TITLE:

_____

DIRECTED BY:

_____

STARRING:

_____

_____

GENRE:

__ drama __ comedy __ romance __ action

__ horror __ sci-fi/fantasy __ foreign __ other

SEE IT:

__ at the theater __ at home

RATING:

__* __** __*** __**** __*****

AWARDS:

deserved: _____

_____

received: _____

_____

[MOVIE REVIEWS]

TITLE:

_____

DIRECTED BY:

_____

STARRING:

_____

_____

GENRE:

__ drama   __ comedy   __ romance   __ action

__ horror   __ sci-fi/fantasy   __ foreign   __ other

SEE IT:

__ at the theater   __ at home

RATING:

__* __** __*** __**** __*****

AWARDS:

deserved: _____

_____

received: _____

_____

[MOVIE REVIEWS]

TITLE:

_____

DIRECTED BY:

_____

STARRING:

_____

_____

GENRE:

__ drama __ comedy __ romance __ action

__ horror __ sci-fi/fantasy __ foreign __ other

SEE IT:

__ at the theater __ at home

RATING:

__* __** __*** __**** __*****

AWARDS:

deserved: _____

_____

received: _____

_____

[MOVIE REVIEWS]

TITLE:

_____

DIRECTED BY:

_____

STARRING:

_____

_____

GENRE:

__ drama __ comedy __ romance __ action

__ horror __ sci-fi/fantasy __ foreign __ other

SEE IT:

__ at the theater __ at home

RATING:

__* __** __*** __**** __*****

AWARDS:

deserved: _____

_____

received: _____

_____

[MOVIE REVIEWS]

TITLE:

_____

DIRECTED BY:

_____

STARRING:

_____

_____

GENRE:

__ drama __ comedy __ romance __ action

__ horror __ sci-fi/fantasy __ foreign __ other

SEE IT:

__ at the theater __ at home

RATING:

__* __** __*** __**** __*****

AWARDS:

deserved: _____

_____

received: _____

_____

[MOVIE REVIEWS]

TITLE:

_____

DIRECTED BY:

_____

STARRING:

_____

_____

GENRE:

__ drama __ comedy __ romance __ action

__ horror __ sci-fi/fantasy __ foreign __ other

SEE IT:

__ at the theater __ at home

RATING:

__* __** __*** __**** __*****

AWARDS:

deserved: _____

_____

received: _____

_____

[MOVIE REVIEWS]

TITLE:

_____

DIRECTED BY:

_____

STARRING:

_____

_____

GENRE:

__ drama __ comedy __ romance __ action

__ horror __ sci-fi/fantasy __ foreign __ other

SEE IT:

__ at the theater __ at home

RATING:

__* __** __*** __**** __*****

AWARDS:

deserved: _____

_____

received: _____

_____

[MOVIE REVIEWS]

TITLE:

_____

DIRECTED BY:

_____

STARRING:

_____

_____

GENRE:

__ drama __ comedy __ romance __ action

__ horror __ sci-fi/fantasy __ foreign __ other

SEE IT:

__ at the theater __ at home

RATING:

__* __** __*** __**** __*****

AWARDS:

deserved: _____

_____

received: _____

_____

[MOVIE REVIEWS]

TITLE:

_____

DIRECTED BY:

_____

STARRING:

_____

_____

GENRE:

__ drama __ comedy __ romance __ action

__ horror __ sci-fi/fantasy __ foreign __ other

SEE IT:

__ at the theater __ at home

RATING:

__* __** __*** __**** __*****

AWARDS:

deserved: _____

_____

received: _____

_____

[MOVIE REVIEWS]

TITLE:

_____

DIRECTED BY:

_____

STARRING:

_____

_____

GENRE:

__ drama __ comedy __ romance __ action

__ horror __ sci-fi/fantasy __ foreign __ other

SEE IT:

__ at the theater __ at home

RATING:

__* __** __*** __**** __*****

AWARDS:

deserved: _____

_____

received: _____

_____

[MOVIE REVIEWS]

TITLE:

_____

DIRECTED BY:

_____

STARRING:

_____

_____

GENRE:

__ drama __ comedy __ romance __ action

__ horror __ sci-fi/fantasy __ foreign __ other

SEE IT:

__ at the theater __ at home

RATING:

__* __** __*** __**** __*****

AWARDS:

deserved: _____

_____

received: _____

_____

[MOVIE REVIEWS]

TITLE:

_____

DIRECTED BY:

_____

STARRING:

_____

_____

GENRE:

__ drama __ comedy __ romance __ action

__ horror __ sci-fi/fantasy __ foreign __ other

SEE IT:

__ at the theater __ at home

RATING:

__* __** __*** __**** __*****

AWARDS:

deserved: _____

_____

received: _____

_____

[MOVIE REVIEWS]

TITLE:

_____

DIRECTED BY:

_____

STARRING:

_____

_____

GENRE:

__ drama __ comedy __ romance __ action

__ horror __ sci-fi/fantasy __ foreign __ other

SEE IT:

__ at the theater __ at home

RATING:

__* __** __*** __**** __*****

AWARDS:

deserved: _____

_____

received: _____

_____

[MOVIE REVIEWS]

TITLE:

_____

DIRECTED BY:

_____

STARRING:

_____

_____

GENRE:

__ drama __ comedy __ romance __ action

__ horror __ sci-fi/fantasy __ foreign __ other

SEE IT:

__ at the theater __ at home

RATING:

__* __** __*** __**** __*****

AWARDS:

deserved: _____

_____

received: _____

_____

[MOVIE REVIEWS]

TITLE:

_____

DIRECTED BY:

_____

STARRING:

_____

_____

GENRE:

__ drama __ comedy __ romance __ action

__ horror __ sci-fi/fantasy __ foreign __ other

SEE IT:

__ at the theater __ at home

RATING:

__* __** __*** __**** __*****

AWARDS:

deserved: _____

_____

received: _____

_____

[MOVIE REVIEWS]

TITLE:

_____

DIRECTED BY:

_____

STARRING:

_____

_____

GENRE:

__ drama __ comedy __ romance __ action

__ horror __ sci-fi/fantasy __ foreign __ other

SEE IT:

__ at the theater __ at home

RATING:

__* __** __*** __**** __*****

AWARDS:

deserved: _____

_____

received: _____

_____

[MOVIE REVIEWS]

TITLE:

_____

DIRECTED BY:

_____

STARRING:

_____

_____

GENRE:

__ drama __ comedy __ romance __ action

__ horror __ sci-fi/fantasy __ foreign __ other

SEE IT:

__ at the theater __ at home

RATING:

__* __** __*** __**** __*****

AWARDS:

deserved: _____

_____

received: _____

_____

[MOVIE REVIEWS]

TITLE:

_____

DIRECTED BY:

_____

STARRING:

_____

_____

GENRE:

__ drama __ comedy __ romance __ action

__ horror __ sci-fi/fantasy __ foreign __ other

SEE IT:

__ at the theater __ at home

RATING:

__* __** __*** __**** __*****

AWARDS:

deserved: _____

_____

received: _____

_____

[MOVIE REVIEWS]

TITLE:

_____

DIRECTED BY:

_____

STARRING:

_____

_____

GENRE:

__ drama __ comedy __ romance __ action

__ horror __ sci-fi/fantasy __ foreign __ other

SEE IT:

__ at the theater __ at home

RATING:

__* __** __*** __**** __*****

AWARDS:

deserved: _____

_____

received: _____

_____

[MOVIE REVIEWS]

TITLE:

_____

DIRECTED BY:

_____

STARRING:

_____

_____

GENRE:

__ drama __ comedy __ romance __ action

__ horror __ sci-fi/fantasy __ foreign __ other

SEE IT:

__ at the theater __ at home

RATING:

__★ __★★ __★★★ __★★★★ __★★★★★

AWARDS:

deserved: _____

_____

received: _____

_____

[MOVIE REVIEWS]

TITLE:

_____

DIRECTED BY:

_____

STARRING:

_____

_____

GENRE:

__ drama __ comedy __ romance __ action

__ horror __ sci-fi/fantasy __ foreign __ other

SEE IT:

__ at the theater __ at home

RATING:

__* __** __*** __**** __*****

AWARDS:

deserved: _____

_____

received: _____

_____

[MOVIE REVIEWS]

TITLE:

_____

DIRECTED BY:

_____

STARRING:

_____

_____

GENRE:

__ drama __ comedy __ romance __ action

__ horror __ sci-fi/fantasy __ foreign __ other

SEE IT:

__ at the theater __ at home

RATING:

__* __** __*** __**** __*****

AWARDS:

deserved: _____

_____

received: _____

_____

[MOVIE REVIEWS]

TITLE:

_____

DIRECTED BY:

_____

STARRING:

_____

_____

GENRE:

__ drama __ comedy __ romance __ action

__ horror __ sci-fi/fantasy __ foreign __ other

SEE IT:

__ at the theater __ at home

RATING:

__* __** __*** __**** __*****

AWARDS:

deserved: _____

_____

received: _____

_____

[MOVIE REVIEWS]

TITLE:

_____

DIRECTED BY:

_____

STARRING:

_____

_____

GENRE:

__ drama __ comedy __ romance __ action

__ horror __ sci-fi/fantasy __ foreign __ other

SEE IT:

__ at the theater __ at home

RATING:

__* __** __*** __**** __*****

AWARDS:

deserved: _____

_____

received: _____

_____

[MOVIE REVIEWS]

TITLE:

_____

DIRECTED BY:

_____

STARRING:

_____

_____

GENRE:

__ drama __ comedy __ romance __ action

__ horror __ sci-fi/fantasy __ foreign __ other

SEE IT:

__ at the theater __ at home

RATING:

__* __** __*** __**** __*****

AWARDS:

deserved: _____

_____

received: _____

_____

[MOVIE REVIEWS]

TITLE:

_____

DIRECTED BY:

_____

STARRING:

_____

_____

GENRE:

__ drama __ comedy __ romance __ action

__ horror __ sci-fi/fantasy __ foreign __ other

SEE IT:

__ at the theater __ at home

RATING:

__* __** __*** __**** __*****

AWARDS:

deserved: _____

_____

received: _____

_____

[MOVIE REVIEWS]

TITLE:

_____

DIRECTED BY:

_____

STARRING:

_____

_____

GENRE:

__ drama __ comedy __ romance __ action

__ horror __ sci-fi/fantasy __ foreign __ other

SEE IT:

__ at the theater __ at home

RATING:

__* __** __*** __**** __*****

AWARDS:

deserved: _____

_____

received: _____

_____

[MOVIE REVIEWS]

TITLE:

_____

DIRECTED BY:

_____

STARRING:

_____

_____

GENRE:

__ drama __ comedy __ romance __ action

__ horror __ sci-fi/fantasy __ foreign __ other

SEE IT:

__ at the theater __ at home

RATING:

__* __** __*** __**** __*****

AWARDS:

deserved: _____

_____

received: _____

_____

[MOVIE REVIEWS]

TITLE:

_____

DIRECTED BY:

_____

STARRING:

_____

_____

GENRE:

__ drama __ comedy __ romance __ action

__ horror __ sci-fi/fantasy __ foreign __ other

SEE IT:

__ at the theater __ at home

RATING:

__* __** __*** __**** __*****

AWARDS:

deserved: _____

_____

received: _____

_____

[MOVIE REVIEWS]

TITLE:

_____

DIRECTED BY:

_____

STARRING:

_____

_____

GENRE:

__ drama __ comedy __ romance __ action

__ horror __ sci-fi/fantasy __ foreign __ other

SEE IT:

__ at the theater __ at home

RATING:

__* __** __*** __**** __*****

AWARDS:

deserved: _____

_____

received: _____

_____

[MOVIE REVIEWS]

TITLE:

_____

DIRECTED BY:

_____

STARRING:

_____

_____

GENRE:

__ drama __ comedy __ romance __ action

__ horror __ sci-fi/fantasy __ foreign __ other

SEE IT:

__ at the theater __ at home

RATING:

__* __** __*** __**** __*****

AWARDS:

deserved: _____

_____

received: _____

_____

[MOVIE REVIEWS]

TITLE:

_____

DIRECTED BY:

_____

STARRING:

_____

_____

GENRE:

__ drama __ comedy __ romance __ action

__ horror __ sci-fi/fantasy __ foreign __ other

SEE IT:

__ at the theater __ at home

RATING:

__* __** __*** __**** __*****

AWARDS:

deserved: _____

_____

received: _____

_____

[MOVIE REVIEWS]

TITLE:

_____

DIRECTED BY:

_____

STARRING:

_____

_____

GENRE:

__ drama __ comedy __ romance __ action

__ horror __ sci-fi/fantasy __ foreign __ other

SEE IT:

__ at the theater __ at home

RATING:

__* __** __*** __**** __*****

AWARDS:

deserved: _____

_____

received: _____

_____

[MOVIE REVIEWS]

TITLE:

_____

DIRECTED BY:

_____

STARRING:

_____

_____

GENRE:

__ drama __ comedy __ romance __ action

__ horror __ sci-fi/fantasy __ foreign __ other

SEE IT:

__ at the theater __ at home

RATING:

__* __** __*** __**** __*****

AWARDS:

deserved: _____

_____

received: _____

_____

[MOVIE REVIEWS]

TITLE:

_____

DIRECTED BY:

_____

STARRING:

_____

_____

GENRE:

__ drama __ comedy __ romance __ action

__ horror __ sci-fi/fantasy __ foreign __ other

SEE IT:

__ at the theater __ at home

RATING:

__* __** __*** __**** __*****

AWARDS:

deserved: _____

_____

received: _____

_____

[MOVIE REVIEWS]

TITLE:

_____

DIRECTED BY:

_____

STARRING:

_____

_____

GENRE:

__ drama __ comedy __ romance __ action

__ horror __ sci-fi/fantasy __ foreign __ other

SEE IT:

__ at the theater __ at home

RATING:

__* __** __*** __**** __*****

AWARDS:

deserved: _____

_____

received: _____

_____

[MOVIE REVIEWS]

TITLE:

_____

DIRECTED BY:

_____

STARRING:

_____

_____

GENRE:

__ drama __ comedy __ romance __ action

__ horror __ sci-fi/fantasy __ foreign __ other

SEE IT:

__ at the theater __ at home

RATING:

__* __** __*** __**** __*****

AWARDS:

deserved: _____

_____

received: _____

_____

[MOVIE REVIEWS]

TITLE:

___

DIRECTED BY:

___

STARRING:

___

___

GENRE:

__ drama __ comedy __ romance __ action

__ horror __ sci-fi/fantasy __ foreign __ other

SEE IT:

__ at the theater __ at home

RATING:

__* __** __*** __**** __*****

AWARDS:

deserved: _____

_____

received: _____

_____

[MOVIE REVIEWS]

TITLE:

_____

DIRECTED BY:

_____

STARRING:

_____

_____

GENRE:

__ drama __ comedy __ romance __ action

__ horror __ sci-fi/fantasy __ foreign __ other

SEE IT:

__ at the theater __ at home

RATING:

__* __** __*** __**** __*****

AWARDS:

deserved: _____

_____

received: _____

_____

[MOVIE REVIEWS]

TITLE:

_____

DIRECTED BY:

_____

STARRING:

_____

_____

GENRE:

__ drama __ comedy __ romance __ action

__ horror __ sci-fi/fantasy __ foreign __ other

SEE IT:

__ at the theater __ at home

RATING:

__* __** __*** __**** __*****

AWARDS:

deserved: _____

_____

received: _____

_____

MY FAVORITES

movies · directors · actors/actresses · scenes · quotes

All I need to make a comedy is a park, a policeman, and a pretty girl.

—CHARLIE CHAPLIN

[MY FAVORITES]

movies • directors • actors/actresses • scenes • quotes

_____

_____

_____

_____

_____

_____

_____

_____

_____

_____

_____

_____

_____

_____

_____

_____

_____

_____

_____

_____

[MY FAVORITES]

movies • directors • actors/actresses • scenes • quotes

_____

_____

_____

_____

_____

_____

_____

_____

_____

_____

_____

_____

_____

_____

_____

_____

_____

_____

_____

_____

_____

[MY FAVORITES]

movies • directors • actors/actresses • scenes • quotes

_____

_____

_____

_____

_____

_____

_____

_____

_____

_____

_____

_____

_____

_____

_____

_____

_____

_____

_____

_____

[MY FAVORITES]

movies • directors • actors/actresses • scenes • quotes

_____

_____

_____

_____

_____

_____

_____

_____

_____

_____

_____

_____

_____

_____

_____

_____

_____

_____

_____

_____

[MY FAVORITES]

movies • directors • actors/actresses • scenes • quotes

_____

_____

_____

_____

_____

_____

_____

_____

_____

_____

_____

_____

_____

_____

_____

_____

_____

_____

_____

[MY FAVORITES]

movies • directors • actors/actresses • scenes • quotes

_____

_____

_____

_____

_____

_____

_____

_____

_____

_____

_____

_____

_____

_____

_____

_____

_____

_____

_____

[MY FAVORITES]

movies • directors • actors/actresses • scenes • quotes

_____

_____

_____

_____

_____

_____

_____

_____

_____

_____

_____

_____

_____

_____

_____

_____

_____

_____

_____

_____

[MY FAVORITES]

movies • directors • actors/actresses • scenes • quotes

_____

_____

_____

_____

_____

_____

_____

_____

_____

_____

_____

_____

_____

_____

_____

_____

_____

_____

_____

_____

[MY FAVORITES]

movies • directors • actors/actresses • scenes • quotes

_____

_____

_____

_____

_____

_____

_____

_____

_____

_____

_____

_____

_____

_____

_____

_____

_____

_____

_____

_____

_____

[MY FAVORITES]

movies • directors • actors/actresses • scenes • quotes

[MY FAVORITES]

movies • directors • actors/actresses • scenes • quotes

_____

_____

_____

_____

_____

_____

_____

_____

_____

_____

_____

_____

_____

_____

_____

_____

_____

_____

_____

_____

[MY FAVORITES]

movies • directors • actors/actresses • scenes • quotes

_____

_____

_____

_____

_____

_____

_____

_____

_____

_____

_____

_____

_____

_____

_____

_____

_____

_____

_____

_____

[MY FAVORITES]

movies • directors • actors/actresses • scenes • quotes

[MY FAVORITES]

movies • directors • actors/actresses • scenes • quotes

_____

_____

_____

_____

_____

_____

_____

_____

_____

_____

_____

_____

_____

_____

_____

_____

_____

_____

_____

_____

_____

[MY FAVORITES]

movies • directors • actors/actresses • scenes • quotes

_____

_____

_____

_____

_____

_____

_____

_____

_____

_____

_____

_____

_____

_____

_____

_____

_____

_____

_____

_____

[MY FAVORITES]

movies • directors • actors/actresses • scenes • quotes

_____

_____

_____

_____

_____

_____

_____

_____

_____

_____

_____

_____

_____

_____

_____

_____

_____

_____

_____

_____

_____

[MY FAVORITES]

movies • directors • actors/actresses • scenes • quotes

_____

_____

_____

_____

_____

_____

_____

_____

_____

_____

_____

_____

_____

_____

_____

_____

_____

_____

_____

_____

[MY FAVORITES]

movies • directors • actors/actresses • scenes • quotes

_____

_____

_____

_____

_____

_____

_____

_____

_____

_____

_____

_____

_____

_____

_____

_____

_____

_____

_____

_____

_____

[MY FAVORITES]

movies • directors • actors/actresses • scenes • quotes

_____

_____

_____

_____

_____

_____

_____

_____

_____

_____

_____

_____

_____

_____

_____

_____

_____

_____

_____

[MY FAVORITES]

movies • directors • actors/actresses • scenes • quotes